KATY
MORGAN

THE

CATALINA
ECHEVERRI

FRIEND

WHO
FORGIVES

15 DAYS EXPLORING THE STORY OF PETER

The Friend Who Forgives Family Bible Devotional
© The Good Book Company, 2023.

Published by:
The Good Book Company

thegoodbook.com | thegoodbook.co.uk
thegoodbook.com.au | thegoodbook.co.nz | thegoodbook.co.in

Design by André Parker | Illustrations from The Friend Who Forgives storybook by Catalina Echeverri

ISBN: 9781784988364 | Printed in India

Contents

Before You Start

Peter messed up again and again, and yet Jesus forgave him. It's easy to summarise the story—and its message is one we all need to know! But it's worth looking deeper into it, too. We can go slowly, notice details along the way and allow this story of friendship and forgiveness to soak into our own lives in a way that changes us. That's true whether we're five or fifty.

Dan DeWitt's storybook *The Friend Who Forgives* is a beautiful, simple retelling of the story of Peter's denial and Jesus's forgiveness. You might have enjoyed it together already, or you might not have seen it at all! Either way, this devotional is a chance to lead your family deeper into the story.

It's designed to be easy to lead and fun to do—and to help your family to grow not just in knowledge of Jesus, but in love for him too.

Each session includes:

- A short opening prayer
- A starter question
- A short Bible passage, printed in full
- Two questions about the passage
- A short explanation that can be read aloud
- Two reflection questions (Usually one is simpler and the other requires more thought. Feel free to just pick one!)
- A final brief thought on the Bible passage, sometimes with an extra question
- A prayer idea

Finally, there's always an optional extra section aimed at older children, if you have them. Sometimes these are based on an extra part of the passage; sometimes they're aiming at deeper reflection. You might like to include these as part of your session, or your child might want to take the book away and look at those sections on their own. Use them however you like!

Some sessions include simple creative reflection ideas. If you have one child, he or she can use the space provided at the end of the chapters for these. But if you have more than one, it's worth having paper and pencils handy.

You'll also find bonus puzzles and colouring activities here and there throughout the book.

I hope these devotions will help your family to explore, reflect and grow together as you enjoy the story of Peter and Jesus. I hope you'll have fun—and I hope you'll see more clearly what Jesus's death on the cross really means for us every day.

1. By the Lake

Pray

Dear Jesus, please teach us about yourself today and make a difference to our lives.

For starters

How well do you know Jesus? Circle the words you might use to talk about him.

teacher   powerful   friend   saviour

master   scary   kind

Luke 5 v 1-5

[1] One day as Jesus was standing by the Lake of Gennesaret, the people were crowding round him and listening to the word of God. [2] He saw at the water's edge two boats, left there by the fishermen, who were washing their nets. [3] He got into one of the boats, the one belonging to Simon, and asked him to put out a little from the shore. Then he sat down and taught the people from the boat.

[4] When he had finished speaking, he said to Simon, "Put out into deep water, and let down the nets for a catch."

[5] Simon answered, "Master, we've worked hard all night and haven't caught anything. But because you say so, I will let down the nets."

Explore the story

Read verses 1-3

Q: *When people listen to Jesus, what are they listening to (v 1)?*

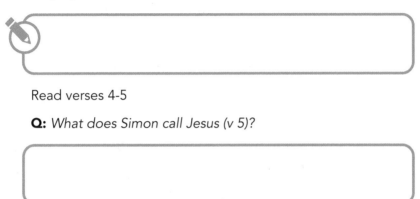

Read verses 4-5

Q: *What does Simon call Jesus (v 5)?*

Simon didn't know Jesus very well yet. But he had heard enough to know that Jesus wasn't just clever or wise. Jesus's words are God's words! Jesus knows what's right. Jesus knows everything! So, it's sensible to let Jesus be in charge. That's what Simon did. He called Jesus "master" and he did what Jesus said.

Later on in the story Simon will be called Peter. You might spot that sometimes he is given both names at once!

Q: *Why do you think it's important to listen to Jesus and do what he says?*

Q: *If we think of Jesus as our master today, what difference do you think that might make to our day?*

Read the story again.

Q: *What do you think is going to happen next?*

⊕ **Extra** ─────────────────────────────

Simon was an expert fisherman, and Jesus wasn't. But Simon didn't say, "In this area of life, I'm the master." No, he did what Jesus said.

Q: *Are there any areas of your life that feel like they don't have anything to do with Jesus?*

Q: *What would it look like for Jesus to be your master in those specific areas?*

Pray

Choose one or two of the words and phrases below and say a prayer that includes those words. Everyone take a turn!

thank you   **Jesus**   **help**   **know**   **please**

teach   **God**   **in charge**   **sorry**

2. A Huge Catch

Pray

Dear Jesus, please teach us about yourself today and make a difference to our lives.

For starters

Put the following things in order from least scary to scariest.

kitten   lion   homework   killer whale

your teacher   singing in front of people

Luke 5 v 5-10a

5 Simon answered, "Master, we've worked hard all night and haven't caught anything. But because you say so, I will let down the nets."

6 When they had done so, they caught such a large number of fish that their nets began to break. 7 So they signalled to their partners in the other boat to come and help them, and they came and filled both boats so full that they began to sink.

8 When Simon Peter saw this, he fell at Jesus' knees and said, "Go away from me, Lord; I am a sinful man!" 9 For he and all his companions were astonished at the catch of fish they had taken, 10 and so were James and John, the sons of Zebedee, Simon's partners.

Explore the story

Read verses 5-10a

Q: *How do the fishermen feel about the catch of fish (v 9)?*

Q: *Why do you think Simon tells Jesus to go away from him (v 8)?*

Jesus had done something amazing. You might think Simon should have jumped up with glee! But instead he fell down in fear. He knew that Jesus was very special—and that he, Simon, wasn't special. In fact, he was sinful. He wasn't good enough to be Jesus's friend. Simon thought that special Jesus should stay away from sinful Simon!

Q: *What are some differences between you and Jesus?*

Q: *What reasons might Jesus have to stay away from us?*

It's right to pause and remember that we are like Simon: sinful. It's not just about how well-behaved we are or aren't. "All have sinned and fall short of the glory of God" (Romans 3 v 23). In other words, none of us are good enough for Jesus! Jesus has no reason to be friends with us. That makes it all the more amazing when we realise that he loves us anyway and is willing to forgive us.

Q: *Think quietly: what is one thing in your life that you know is sinful and not right? Maybe you've hurt someone else, or you've been disobedient. Maybe there's some other way in which you haven't been treating Jesus as the master of your life.*

Ask Jesus for forgiveness now. Write down your prayer if you like.

Read the story again.

Q: *Can you think of one word that you would use to describe Jesus in this story?*

In the next study we will see that Jesus didn't go away from Simon. In fact, he did the opposite…

Pray

Use your answers to the final question to make this prayer your own.

Dear Jesus, you are [*add your own words here*]. You are special and we are sinful. We could never be as special and wonderful as you! Thank you that you want to come close to us and love us anyway.

3. From Now On

Pray
Dear Jesus, please teach us about yourself today and make a difference to our lives.

For starters
What are some things you do every day?

Pick two of those things. On a scale of one to ten, how much would you like to leave each thing behind and stop doing it?

(1 = I wouldn't like to stop this thing at all! 10 = Yes please, can I stop today?)

Luke 5 v 9-11
[9] [Simon] and all his companions were astonished at the catch of fish they had taken, [10] and so were James and John, the sons of Zebedee, Simon's partners. Then Jesus said to Simon, "Don't be afraid; from now on you will fish for people." [11] So they pulled their boats up on shore, left everything and followed him.

Explore the story
Read verses 9-11

Q: *Does Jesus want Simon to be scared of him?*

Q: *What do Simon and his friends leave everything for?*

Simon thought Jesus should leave. But instead, Simon ended up leaving—with Jesus! Simon was sinful, but Jesus had a job for him to do. Simon was going to fish for people, not fish! That meant he was going to help Jesus search for other sinful people—people who needed forgiveness. Simon left everything to be part of Jesus's mission. He left behind things he liked as well as things he didn't like. He put Jesus first.

Q: *Fishing for fish was less important to Simon than following Jesus. Can you think of some things you like doing that are less important than following Jesus?*

Q: *Putting Jesus first sometimes means giving things up. If someone today wants to put Jesus first, what changes might they make in their lives?*

Read the story again.

Q: *How do you think Simon and his friends felt as they left the beach with Jesus?*

From now on, Simon stops being called Simon and starts being called Peter. Peter means "rock"!

+ Extra

Simon was going to learn about fishing for people. We can fish for people today too. That just means telling them about Jesus and about Jesus's forgiveness.

Think of three friends you'll see this week who don't know Jesus yet.

Q: *What is one thing you could tell each of them about Jesus this week—or even today?*

Pray that God will give you a chance to be a fisher of people.

Pray

Draw a big footprint. You're going to fill it with some things that are important in your life.

First of all, write the name JESUS inside your foot shape.

Think about how big or small you want to make his name: how big a part of your life is he, or how big a part of your life would you like him to be?

Then surround the name with words or drawings that show some other things that are important in your life.

You might also like to say this prayer.

Dear Jesus, thank you for things I love, like [*add your own words here*]. But following you is more important than anything else. I want to put you first. Please help me to be thankful for the things you've given me, but also to be ready to give them up if you want me to.

Every so often in this book you'll find colouring and activity pages like these ones. Have fun getting creative and solving the puzzles!

Wordsearch

h	k	i	g	b	g	s	c	f	i	s	a	j	d	u
g	t	a	t	n	i	f	s	a	i	l	q	b	i	y
e	k	h	o	i	f	r	t	h	t	o	r	g	b	d
l	w	r	i	a	s	w	e	s	l	c	n	e	f	v
e	t	e	d	n	o	r	s	b	g	i	h	o	r	t
s	e	o	i	e	k	k	r	p	t	g	l	d	i	b
r	d	e	m	e	k	e	y	m	e	r	s	u	e	k
i	o	b	o	a	t	n	o	d	l	a	i	d	n	a
l	k	h	u	e	n	o	e	l	e	k	k	e	d	w
a	l	x	p	f	b	c	k	s	h	a	s	c	p	n
i	v	g	g	e	s	u	j	e	s	u	s	m	y	d
a	i	i	p	h	o	b	w	p	i	e	a	s	k	w
e	b	r	s	e	n	p	s	g	f	s	i	o	i	n
z	o	n	e	t	h	e	l	o	y	e	j	g	i	l
s	u	e	j	e	s	u	x	b	r	a	v	e	f	a

- [ ] Peter
- [ ] fish
- [ ] boat
- [ ] catch
- [ ] net
- [ ] friend
- [ ] strong
- [ ] brave
- [ ] speak
- [ ] think
- [ ] sail
- [ ] Jesus

Pray

Dear Jesus, thank you for who you are. We want to be amazed by you today!

For starters

What's the most amazing thing you've ever seen?

Matthew 8 v 14-17

14 When Jesus came into Peter's house, he saw Peter's mother-in-law lying in bed with a fever. 15 He touched her hand and the fever left her, and she got up and began to wait on him.

16 When evening came, many who were demon-possessed were brought to him, and he drove out the spirits with a word and healed all who were ill. 17 This was to fulfil what was spoken through the prophet Isaiah:

"He took up our infirmities
and bore our diseases."

Explore the story

Read verses 14-16

Q: *What does Jesus do in order to heal people (v 15, 16)?*

Q: *Why do lots of people come to Jesus (v 16)?*

Simon Peter saw Jesus do lots of amazing things. Jesus wasn't just a wise teacher. He cared about people and he wanted to help them—and he did help them! Jesus healed people with just one touch or just one word. He made people free from evil. Jesus could do anything!

 Extra ——————————————————————
Read verse 17

"Infirmities" means "weaknesses". "Bore" means "carried".

The prophet Isaiah was a messenger from God who lived hundreds of years before Jesus. He spoke about Jesus in advance.

Q: *Isaiah didn't just say that Jesus would get rid of people's diseases—what did he say he would do with them?*

This is a hint at what Jesus was going to do later, on the cross. Jesus didn't just suffer: he took our suffering. All people have sinned—that means we have turned away from God. Our sin causes suffering in lots of different ways. But Jesus died to take away our sin and our suffering. One day, after we die, Jesus's followers will experience no more pain, disease or unhappiness.

Q: *What would you like to ask Jesus to do for you or for someone else today?*

Q: *Can you think of some situations when it's especially important for us to remember that Jesus can do anything?*

Read the story again.

Q: *Lots of people were coming to see Jesus. What do you think they thought of him?*

Pray

Share one thing each that you'd like Jesus to help you with. Then say a short prayer for each other. Your prayer might sound something like this:

Dear Jesus, I pray for [family member]. Please help them to [get well soon / sleep well / get along with someone better / be more thankful / etc!].

It might help to write your prayers down so that you can remember what you've prayed for and see how Jesus answers your prayers.

5. A Furious Storm

Pray
Dear Jesus, thank you for who you are. We want to be amazed by you today!

For starters
Draw the scariest, biggest storm you can. Use the space on page 27 if you like, or a separate sheet of paper. You have 60 seconds. Go! (You'll come back to this at the end…)

Matthew 8 v 23-27
23 Then [Jesus] got into the boat and his disciples followed him. 24 Suddenly a furious storm came up on the lake, so that the waves swept over the boat. But Jesus was sleeping. 25 The disciples went and woke him, saying, "Lord, save us! We're going to drown!"

26 He replied, "You of little faith, why are you so afraid?" Then he got up and rebuked the winds and the waves, and it was completely calm.

27 The men were amazed and asked, "What kind of man is this? Even the winds and the waves obey him!"

Explore the story
Read verses 23-25

Q: *Why are the disciples so afraid?*

Read verses 26-27

Q: *What are they wondering about Jesus? Why?*

The wind was strong, the waves were tall, and the disciples thought they were going to drown! But Jesus just stood up and told the storm off—and it calmed down. How amazing! Peter and the other disciples never needed to be afraid at all, not when they had Jesus in the boat with them. Now the disciples were realising that Jesus is stronger than any storm. But how could any man be as powerful as *that*?

⊕ Extra ────────────────────

Jesus said the disciples had "little faith" (v 26). That means they didn't trust Jesus as much as they could have done.

Q: *What might they have done if they had had more faith in Jesus?*

Q: *What might they have done if they had had less faith in Jesus?*

Q: *Think quietly: how do you think you would have acted in this situation? Be honest!*

Q: *If we know Jesus is with us, do we need to be afraid? Why or why not?*

Q: *Think of something specific that sometimes makes you feel afraid. When you're facing that thing, how could it help to remember what Jesus is like?*

Read the story again.

Q: *How would you answer the disciples' question in verse 27?*

Pray
Using the picture you drew at the start, add two stick figures to represent yourself and Jesus.

Next to the figure of yourself, write the words, "Lord, save us!" As you do, think about a situation you are facing that is scary or overwhelming and ask for Jesus's help.

Then, next to the Jesus figure, write the words, "Why are you so afraid?" As you do, thank Jesus for the fact that you don't have to be afraid, because he is stronger than any scary thing.

6. Who Is Jesus?

Pray

Dear Jesus, thank you for who you are. We want to be amazed by you today!

For starters

How would you treat a friend differently from a queen or king?

How would you treat a brother or sister differently from a teacher?

Matthew 16 v 13-17

¹³ When Jesus came to the region of Caesarea Philippi, he asked his disciples, "Who do people say the Son of Man is?"

¹⁴ They replied, "Some say John the Baptist; others say Elijah; and still others, Jeremiah or one of the prophets."

¹⁵ "But what about you?" he asked. "Who do you say I am?"

¹⁶ Simon Peter answered, "You are the Messiah, the Son of the living God."

¹⁷ Jesus replied, "Blessed are you, Simon son of Jonah, for this was not revealed to you by flesh and blood, but by my Father in heaven."

Explore the story

Read verses 13-16

Q: *Who does Peter say that Jesus is (v 16)?*

Q: *What ideas do other people have about who Jesus is (v 14)?*

John the Baptist, Elijah and Jeremiah were all prophets: messengers sent by God to his people. Some people thought that Jesus must be a prophet too. But Peter realised that Jesus wasn't just a prophet. Jesus was the Messiah (or Christ): the King whom God had promised to send. And he hadn't just been *sent* by God; he was the *Son* of God.

Q: *What have we heard about so far in Peter's story that has shown us who Jesus really is?*

Q: *How do you think someone would treat Jesus if they thought he was a prophet? How would they treat him differently if they knew he was God's Son? Why?*

Extra

Read verse 17

Q: *How did Peter know who Jesus was?*

Lots of people today don't know who Jesus is. It's important for us to tell them! But in the end, they'll only find out the truth if God reveals it to them. God has to change people's hearts and open their eyes in order for them to realise that Jesus is God's Son. So we need to pray that he will do that for the people we are telling about Jesus.

Q: *Think of some friends who don't know Jesus. Could you commit to praying for one or two of them every day this week?*

Read the story again.

Jesus was Peter's friend—but he was also more than that. Jesus was amazing, powerful and the Son of God!

Pray

How many words can you think of that describe what Jesus is like? See if you can come up with a prayer of praise that includes all those words! Or, take turns to say, "Thank you Jesus that you are [*special / powerful / amazing / etc*]." Keep going until you run out of words.

Pray

Dear Jesus, thank you that you came to earth for us. Please speak to us today and help us know you better.

For starters

Which of the following feelings would you most like to feel? Which would you least like to feel?

loved and looked-after   **afraid you might die**

excited about a party   **worried you've let someone down**

like you have no friends   **proud of having done well**

Matthew 26 v 30-35

30 When [Jesus and his disciples] had sung a hymn, they went out to the Mount of Olives.

31 Then Jesus told them, "This very night you will all fall away on account of me, for it is written:

'I will strike the shepherd,
    and the sheep of the flock will be scattered.'

32 But after I have risen, I will go ahead of you into Galilee."

33 Peter replied, "Even if all fall away on account of you, I never will."

³⁴ "Truly I tell you," Jesus answered, "this very night, before the rooster crows, you will disown me three times."

³⁵ But Peter declared, "Even if I have to die with you, I will never disown you." And all the other disciples said the same.

Explore the story
Read verses 30-35

Q: *What does Jesus say the disciples will do (v 31)?*

Q: *What does Peter think about that (v 33, 35)?*

Jesus has just explained that he is going to be arrested and then killed. When Jesus gets arrested, his disciples are going to be so scared that they'll say they're not Jesus's friends. When Peter hears this, he speaks up right away: *I will never do that!* Jesus is Peter's best friend—of course Peter won't let Jesus down. At least, that's what he thinks…

Q: *Letting people down is always bad. Why do you think letting Jesus down is even more of a big deal?*

Q: *If Peter lets Jesus down, how do you think he will feel?*

⊕ Extra

Jesus warned his friends that they would let him down. Sadly, Jesus's friends still let Jesus down today. We act like we don't know him. We disobey him. Or we don't put him first in our lives.

Q: *Can you think of some specific ways in which Christians might let Jesus down today—at home, at school, in the playground, at a friend's house?*

The truth is that none of us are good enough friends to Jesus. We can only be good friends to him if he helps us. We need to pray for his help!

Read the story again.

Who is right—Jesus or Peter? Soon we'll find out. It's starting to get dark...

Pray

Jesus knows everything we'll do that's bad—and he still chooses to be our friend. He is a much better friend to us than we could ever be to him!

Say or write a thank-you prayer to celebrate Jesus's friendship. You might also want to add some sorry prayers about times when you have let Jesus or other people down. And you might want to ask God to help you be a better friend to Jesus in the future.

Pray

Dear Jesus, thank you that you came to earth for us. Please speak to us today and help us know you better.

For starters

Imagine the following situations. If these things happened, would they make you trust or not trust the person in the future?

Your friend saves you a cake when you're late to her party.

Your friend tells you that you can sit next to him on the bus, but then he sits next to someone else.

Someone asks to borrow something and then gives it back later the same day.

John 18 v 1-5

¹ When he had finished praying, Jesus left with his disciples and crossed the Kidron Valley. On the other side there was a garden, and he and his disciples went into it.

² Now Judas, who betrayed him, knew the place, because Jesus had often met there with his disciples. ³ So Judas came to the garden, guiding a detachment of soldiers and some officials from the chief priests and the Pharisees. They were carrying torches, lanterns and weapons.

⁴ Jesus, knowing all that was going to happen to him, went out and asked them, "Who is it you want?"

⁵ "Jesus of Nazareth," they replied.

"I am he," Jesus said. (And Judas the traitor was standing there with them.)

Explore the story

Read verses 1-3

Q: *What do the men bring with them (v 3)? What do you think is going to happen?*

Read verses 4-5

Q: *Jesus knows what the men are there for. He goes out to meet them and tells them who he is. Would you have done that?*

Judas was one of Jesus's friends—except he wasn't anymore. Judas knew that the chief priests wanted Jesus to die. So Judas told them where to find Jesus. Here the soldiers came, through the garden, in the dark… And Jesus was ready for them. But he didn't run away or fight back—he let himself be arrested! Jesus knew that he had to die on the cross in order to offer people forgiveness. The soldiers were scary, but they were part of his plan.

Q: *Jesus was ready to be arrested and then die—for us! How does that make you feel?*

Q: *Jesus always knows what's going to happen (v 4). How does that make you feel?*

(+) Extra ────────────────────────────

Q: *Can you think of a time when you knew what the right thing to do was, but you were scared about doing it?*

The first verse of our story today tells us that Jesus had been praying. He prayed for help from God to go through with the plan (Matthew 26 v 39, 42). Even Jesus needed to pray for God's help to do hard things.

Jesus also prayed specifically for you (John 17 v 20-26)—and he is still praying for you, right now. So, the next time you find it hard to be a follower of Jesus, you can be confident to ask him for help!

Try writing a short prayer now that you could remember for the future.

Read the story again.

Jesus was ready to be arrested. But Peter was about to take matters into his own hands…

Pray

Has Jesus earned your trust? Write the words I TRUST YOU JESUS in bubble-writing and colour them in. As you do, talk together about situations where you will need Jesus's help this week. When you've finished colouring, ask Jesus to help you with those things.

Pray

Dear Jesus, thank you that you came to earth for us. Please speak to us today and help us know you better.

For starters

Can you think of a time when you've disagreed about what the best thing to do is? Who wanted to do what? How did you solve the disagreement?

John 18 v 10-14

[10] Then Simon Peter, who had a sword, drew it and struck the high priest's servant, cutting off his right ear. (The servant's name was Malchus.)

[11] Jesus commanded Peter, "Put your sword away! Shall I not drink the cup the Father has given me?"

[12] Then the detachment of soldiers with its commander and the Jewish officials arrested Jesus. They bound him [13] and brought him first to Annas, who was the father-in-law of Caiaphas, the high priest that year. [14] Caiaphas was the one who had advised the Jewish leaders that it would be good if one man died for the people.

Explore the story

Read verse 10

Q: *How does Peter try to stop Jesus getting arrested?*

Read verses 11-12 (up to "arrested Jesus")

Q: *What phrase does Jesus use that means "God's plan for me"?*

 Extra ─────────────────────────

Read verses 12-14

Q: *What has Caiaphas said about Jesus's death (v 14)?*

The Jewish leaders had been worrying that Jesus would try to throw out the Romans, who were in charge, and become king instead. The Romans would kill lots of people if the Jews tried to make Jesus their king. So Caiaphas thought that, if Jesus died, it would save lots of other people from being killed.

Caiaphas didn't realise it, but he'd actually put his finger on something very important about Jesus's death. Jesus *was* going to die for the people. Jesus's plan was to die on the cross so that people could be forgiven and have eternal life.

Peter didn't want Jesus to die! But Jesus knew that he *had* to die. That was God's plan for bringing forgiveness to people. When we turn away from Jesus, we don't deserve Jesus's friendship. We deserve punishment. This is true for all of us— we all turn away from Jesus in one way or another! But Jesus took our "cup" of punishment *for* us. He died so that we don't have to be punished. Instead we can be forgiven and become friends with God. Peter didn't understand that Jesus's death was God's plan for forgiveness.

Q: *Why is it better to follow God's plans than our own plans?*

Q: *Could you explain God's plan for Jesus in your own words? What questions do you have about it?*

Read the story again.

Q: *How do you think Peter felt as he watched Jesus being led away?*

Pray

Draw a cross and write a prayer on it praising Jesus for being willing to die so that we could have forgiveness. Use at least two of the following words and phrases:

Jesus   **died**   **sorry**   **thank you**   **God**   **sin**

forgiven   **plan**   **amazing**   **trust**

10. The Rooster Crows

Pray

Dear Jesus, thank you that you came to earth for us. Please speak to us today and help us know you better.

For starters

When you've done something wrong, how do you feel? Choose as many answers as you like from this list, or add your own.

happy   guilty   sad   worried   peaceful

angry   upset   silly

Luke 22 v 54-62

54 Then seizing him, they led him away and took him into the house of the high priest. Peter followed at a distance. 55 And when some there had kindled a fire in the middle of the courtyard and had sat down together, Peter sat down with them. 56 A servant-girl saw him seated there in the firelight. She looked closely at him and said, "This man was with him."

57 But he denied it. "Woman, I don't know him," he said.

58 A little later someone else saw him and said, "You also are one of them."

"Man, I am not!" Peter replied.

⁵⁹ About an hour later another asserted, "Certainly this fellow was with him, for he is a Galilean."

⁶⁰ Peter replied, "Man, I don't know what you're talking about!" Just as he was speaking, the rooster crowed. ⁶¹ The Lord turned and looked straight at Peter. Then Peter remembered the word the Lord had spoken to him: "Before the rooster crows today, you will disown me three times." ⁶² And he went outside and wept bitterly.

Explore the story
Read verses 54-60

Q: *How many times does Peter say he doesn't know Jesus?*

Read verses 61-62

Q: *Why does Peter weep bitterly?*

Jesus was Peter's friend—the best friend ever! So surely Peter could NEVER let Jesus down. Or could he? Yes. *I don't know Jesus,* he told people—three times. Then the rooster crowed. Oh no! This was exactly what Jesus had predicted. Peter had been so sure that he would never let Jesus down. But instead he had failed Jesus again, and again, and again.

Q: *Imagine your best friend pretended they didn't know you, just like Peter did to Jesus. How would you react?*

Q: *What would someone be like if they were the best possible friend to Jesus? Do you think it's possible for anyone to be like that?*

⊕ **Extra**

Just like Peter, it's easy for us to think that we'll never let Jesus down. But the truth is that all of us let Jesus down.

Whenever we fail to put Jesus first, we are letting him down. Whenever we forget to talk to him in prayer, or choose to do something we know he wouldn't like, we are letting him down. Whenever we think we're doing all right on our own and forget how much we need Jesus, we are letting him down.

Q: *Think quietly. Are there any ways in which you've let Jesus down recently—big or small? Say sorry to him now in prayer.*

Read the story again.

Peter felt terrible. Could he ever be forgiven? Peter didn't understand it yet, but the answer would be YES. Jesus came to give forgiveness to friends who let him down. In fact, bringing forgiveness was exactly what Jesus was going to die for.

Pray

Use scraps of paper to write down or draw one or two things that you've done that you're sorry about—or that you wish you had done but you didn't! Then say this prayer together:

Jesus, thank you for dying so that we can be forgiven. Thank you for being our Lord and Saviour. We're sorry for what we've done wrong. Please forgive us. Please help us to be better friends to you in the future. Please help us to be better friends to the people we've hurt, too.

Then screw up the papers and throw them in the bin. If you prayed that prayer, then Jesus forgives you! Those sins are now done with. Say thank you to God!

Spot the difference

Can you spot the five differences between these two pictures?

Join the dots

11. Gone

Pray

Dear Jesus, we love you and we need you. Please remind us of your nearness today.

For starters

Do you like surprises? What's the best surprise you've ever had?

John 20 v 1-10

[1] Early on the first day of the week, while it was still dark, Mary Magdalene went to the tomb and saw that the stone had been removed from the entrance. [2] So she came running to Simon Peter and the other disciple, the one Jesus loved, and said, "They have taken the Lord out of the tomb, and we don't know where they have put him!"

[3] So Peter and the other disciple started for the tomb. [4] Both were running, but the other disciple outran Peter and reached the tomb first. [5] He bent over and looked in at the strips of linen lying there but did not go in. [6] Then Simon Peter came along behind him and went straight into the tomb. He saw the strips of linen lying there, [7] as well as the cloth that had been wrapped round Jesus' head. The cloth was still lying in its place, separate from the linen. [8] Finally the other disciple, who had reached the tomb first, also went inside. He saw and believed. [9] (They still did not understand from Scripture that Jesus had to rise from the dead.) [10] Then the disciples went back to where they were staying.

Explore the story

Read verses 1-2

Q: *What was Mary expecting to see in the tomb?*

```

```

Read verses 3-10

Q: *What does Peter see in the tomb?*

```

```

Just as he planned, Jesus died. But he didn't stay dead. Three days after Jesus died came the first Easter Sunday. Jesus's body had been put into a tomb, but now the tomb was empty! What had happened? Could it be that Jesus had risen from the dead? Yes! Jesus's resurrection proved that Jesus was God's Son. And it proved that God's plan had worked. The punishment for all our sins was now complete—and it had all been taken by Jesus.

⊕ Extra ─────────────────────

Peter hadn't understood that the Old Testament predicted that Jesus would rise again (v 9). Later he would realise that this was what Psalm 16 was about. (He gave a whole speech about this in Acts 2 v 22-36!)

Find Psalm 16 in your Bible and read verses 9-11. (The "me" in this psalm is Jesus. The "you" is God the Father.)

Q: *What will God not allow to happen to Jesus (v 10)?*

Q: *What will he give him instead (v 11)?*

Q: *Why do you think it's important that God promised Jesus's death and resurrection in advance?*

Q: *Why were Jesus's friends so surprised when Jesus rose from the dead?*

Q: *Why do you think it's important for us to know that Jesus rose from the dead? (Hint: What does it tell us about him? What does it tell us about what's happened to our sin?)*

Read the story again.

Jesus was back from the dead. But would he forgive Peter for failing him so badly?

Pray

Invent your own thank-you prayer to Jesus. Include the words "rose from the dead". Finish your prayer with these words:

Please help us to believe that you rose from the dead and that you really are God's Son. Amen.

12. Fish for Breakfast

Pray
Dear Jesus, we love you and we need you. Please remind us of your nearness today.

For starters
For each of these problems (in orange), choose the thing you need (in green).

food spilled on your clothes   a spelling mistake

you've upset your friend

an eraser   the word "sorry"   a washing machine

John 21 v 4-13

4 Early in the morning, Jesus stood on the shore, but the disciples did not realise that it was Jesus.

5 He called out to them, "Friends, haven't you any fish?"

"No," they answered.

6 He said, "Throw your net on the right side of the boat and you will find some." When they did, they were unable to haul the net in because of the large number of fish.

7 Then the disciple whom Jesus loved said to Peter, "It is the Lord!" As soon as Simon Peter heard him say, "It is the Lord," he wrapped his outer garment round him (for he had taken it off) and jumped into the water. 8 The other disciples followed in the boat, towing the net full of fish, for they were not far from shore, about a hundred metres.

⁹ When they landed, they saw a fire of burning coals there with fish on it, and some bread.

¹⁰ Jesus said to them, "Bring some of the fish you have just caught." ¹¹ So Simon Peter climbed back into the boat and dragged the net ashore. It was full of large fish, 153, but even with so many the net was not torn. ¹² Jesus said to them, "Come and have breakfast." None of the disciples dared ask him, "Who are you?" They knew it was the Lord. ¹³ Jesus came, took the bread and gave it to them, and did the same with the fish.

Explore the story

Not long after Jesus has risen from the dead, Peter and some of the other disciples are fishing.

Read verses 4-13

Q: *What do you think makes the disciples recognise Jesus?*

Q: *Why do you think Peter jumps into the water?*

Does this story remind you of anything? It's like we're back at the start. Peter was fishing when he met Jesus for the first time, too—and not catching anything. But when Jesus told him what to do, he caught lots of fish. Now the same thing has happened again. A new day is starting. Maybe this can be a new start for Peter. Maybe it can be a new start for his friendship with Jesus.

Q: *Imagine you had one of the problems we talked about at the start. If it was solved, how would you feel?*

Q: *What would it feel like for someone today to be forgiven by Jesus? Why?*

⊕ Extra

Look back at verses 7-8. The disciples were only 100 metres from the land—they would reach Jesus soon! But "soon" wasn't fast enough for Peter.

Some people do the opposite to what Peter did. When they have messed up, they run away from Jesus—they stop praying and wanting him to be in their lives. They pretend he isn't there.

Q: *Can you think why someone might do that?*

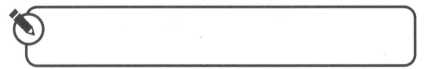

Q: *Why is it always better to run to Jesus?*

Read the story again.

Peter was so happy to see Jesus alive, but would Jesus forgive him?

Pray

Choose the prayer that's right for you today, or invent your own. Say it out loud or in your head.

Dear Jesus, I love you. I want to get closer to you! Please show me how and teach me how to be your follower.

Dear Jesus, you are amazing, but I don't know if I can follow you like you want. Please help me.

Dear Jesus, I'm so glad I'm your friend and you've forgiven me. Please help me never to stop being close to you!

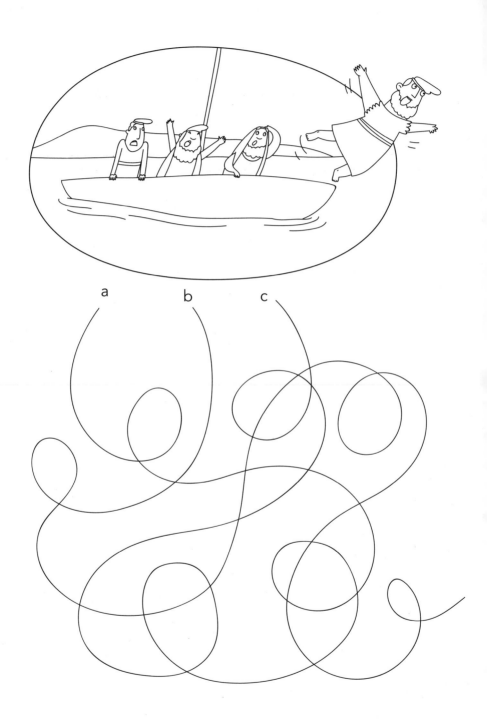

a   b   c

Find the right route to get Peter to the shore! Then colour in his breakfast with Jesus.

13. Feeding Sheep

Pray
Dear Jesus, we love you and we need you. Please remind us of your nearness today.

For starters
Invent a recipe for a special food that is more filling, nourishing and delicious than anything else. What ingredients would you include?

John 21 v 15-17

15 When they had finished eating, Jesus said to Simon Peter, "Simon son of John, do you love me more than these?"

"Yes, Lord," he said, "you know that I love you."

Jesus said, "Feed my lambs."

16 Again Jesus said, "Simon son of John, do you love me?"

He answered, "Yes, Lord, you know that I love you."

Jesus said, 'Take care of my sheep.'

17 The third time he said to him, "Simon son of John, do you love me?"

Peter was hurt because Jesus asked him the third time, "Do you love me?"

He said, "Lord, you know all things; you know that I love you."

Jesus said, "Feed my sheep."

Explore the story

Read verses 15-17

Q: *What does Simon Peter say three times?*

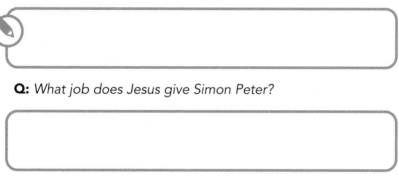

Q: *What job does Jesus give Simon Peter?*

Would Jesus forgive Peter? Yes! Since Peter had said he didn't know Jesus three times, Jesus gave Peter the chance to say three times, "I love you." Then Jesus showed Peter that he was still his friend by giving him a job to do. It was similar to the job Jesus gave Peter before. Peter was going to find people who needed forgiveness and tell them about Jesus. Not just that: he was going to help them to follow Jesus. The truth about Jesus is like food for hungry sheep!

Q: *How do you think Peter might have felt about his new start?*

Q: *Which do you think is more important: Our love for Jesus or Jesus's love for us? What we do for Jesus or what Jesus has done for us?*

⊕ Extra ─────────────────────────────

Sometimes we think we have to do things to earn forgiveness from God. We have to be really good, and then he'll love us. But Peter's story shows us that that's not true. Peter had failed Jesus again and again and again. But Jesus forgave him—and then gave him a job to do. The good works came after the forgiveness, not the other way around.

Q: *This week, what is one good thing you could do—maybe something to help someone to follow Jesus?*

Whatever you decide to do, start by saying, "Jesus, thank you for loving me even though I don't deserve it. I love you too." This will help you to remember that Jesus loved you already, before you did anything good!

Read the story again.

Q: *What do you think Peter will do next?*

Pray

Think of people you know who need to be reminded of the truth about Jesus. Maybe they are worried about something and they need to remember that Jesus is with them. Or they are feeling unloved and they need to remember that Jesus died for them. Or they are sick or sad and they need to remember that Jesus is going to make everything new one day.

What is one thing you can do to remind each of those people of the truth about Jesus?

Start by praying for them!

14. A Strange Sound

Pray

Dear Jesus, you're the greatest friend we could ever have. Please speak to us by your Spirit and help us follow you today.

For starters

What could the following things help you to do?

a squeezy stress ball   **a torch**   **a French dictionary**

a guide to friendship   **very good sports shoes**

Acts 1 v 8-9; 2 v 1-4

8 [Jesus said,] "But you will receive power when the Holy Spirit comes on you; and you will be my witnesses in Jerusalem, and in all Judea and Samaria, and to the ends of the earth.'

9 After he said this, he was taken up before their very eyes, and a cloud hid him from their sight ...

2 v 1 When the day of Pentecost came, they were all together in one place. 2 Suddenly a sound like the blowing of a violent wind came from heaven and filled the whole house where they were sitting. 3 They saw what seemed to be tongues of fire that separated and came to rest on each of them. 4 All of them were filled with the Holy Spirit and began to speak in other tongues as the Spirit enabled them.

Explore the story

Read chapter 1 verses 8-9

Q: *Jesus is speaking to his disciples. What does he tell them they will do?*

Read chapter 2 verses 1-4

Q: *What does the Holy Spirit enable the disciples to do?*

Peter and the other disciples were going to tell people about Jesus—but not on their own. God's Spirit came to help them. Suddenly the disciples found themselves speaking other languages! Now they could tell everyone in the world about Jesus. Today the Holy Spirit lives in everyone who puts their trust in Jesus. He might not make us speak other languages, but he will definitely remind us about Jesus and help us tell others.

Q: *What could you ask God's Spirit for help with this week?*

Q: *How do you feel about telling people about Jesus? What difference does it make to know that the Spirit can help?*

Extra

The Holy Spirit empowers us to be Jesus's witnesses: to tell people about Jesus and show them what he's like. And that's just the start.

Find and read the following verses to see some of the things the Spirit does in and through us. Match each passage (in orange) to one of the summaries below (in green).

Romans 8 v 15-16   Galatians 5 v 22-23

1 Corinthians 12 v 7-10

The Spirit changes the way we live

The Spirit gives us gifts to help us encourage others

The Spirit reminds us that we're God's children and helps us to pray

Q: *What is one thing you'd like the Spirit to do in your life?*

Q: *How could that help you be a witness of Jesus?*

Read the story again.

As the disciples burst out with different languages, people stopped to listen. People from all over the world were hearing about Jesus!

Pray

Share one thing each that you would like to do or say this week that would help someone find out about how wonderful Jesus is. Write them in the box below. Then pray for each other, asking God for his help to do that.

15. Peter's Message

Pray

Dear Jesus, you're the greatest friend we could ever have. Please speak to us by your Spirit and help us follow you today.

For starters

Which of these pieces of news would you be happiest to hear?

Your birthday party has been cancelled.

The friend you hurt isn't mad with you after all.

It's raining.

You're going to spend the weekend with your best friend.

Acts 2 v 38-41

[38] Peter replied, "Repent and be baptised, every one of you, in the name of Jesus Christ for the forgiveness of your sins. And you will receive the gift of the Holy Spirit. [39] The promise is for you and your children and for all who are far off—for all whom the Lord our God will call."

[40] With many other words he warned them; and he pleaded with them, "Save yourselves from this corrupt generation." [41] Those who accepted his message were baptised, and about three thousand were added to their number that day.

Explore the story

Peter has been telling people all about Jesus.

Read verses 38-39

Q: *Who can receive forgiveness and the Holy Spirit?*

Read verses 40-41

Q: *How do people respond to Peter's message?*

This was just the start. Peter spent the rest of his life telling people about his best friend, Jesus. He told them that if they turned away from what they had done wrong and put their trust in Jesus, then Jesus would forgive them—again, and again, and again. Jesus would be their friend and the Holy Spirit would help them to follow him. Peter's amazing news spread… and spread… and spread!

Q: *When we have let Jesus down, what should we do?*

Q: *Peter tells us to ask God for forgiveness "in the name of Jesus Christ". Why do we need Jesus in order to be forgiven?*

> [blank box]

⊕ Extra

Peter said, "Repent and be baptised" (v 38). "Repent" means "turn away from sin". When we turn away from our sin and put our trust in Jesus, Jesus washes us clean from sin and gives us a new start. Being baptised is a way of showing that this has happened to you. Sometimes being baptised means being dunked in a pool of water, or even a river or the sea! Sometimes it means your head being sprinkled with water. Baptism is a sign that Jesus has forgiven you and given you his Holy Spirit.

Some people are baptised as children, while others wait until they are older and more certain about their faith. Whether or not you've been baptised, you can still turn away from sin and put your trust in Jesus each day.

Have you done that? Make a sign that you can put up somewhere to remind you that Jesus has given you a new start. Or use the box on the page opposite. Be as creative as you like!

Read the story again.

Peter's message is still spreading. All over the world, there are people who know Jesus as their friend who forgives. I wonder where the message will go next…

Pray

Read the prayer below together, or invent your own prayers as you respond to this story. Start with "In the name of Jesus Christ" and make sure you include the words "thank you"!

In the name of Jesus Christ, we repent of our sins and we ask for forgiveness. Jesus, please wash us clean and give us a new start. Please give us your Holy Spirit and help us to follow you. Please give us words to share your message, just like Peter did. Thank you for being the greatest friend we could ever have.

Finish this picture by adding lots of people listening to Peter's message about Jesus.

Match the shadows

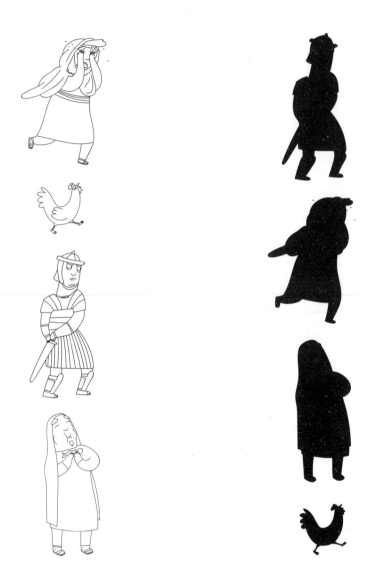

These people are all from the story. Can you match them to their shadows?

thegoodbook
COMPANY

BIBLICAL | RELEVANT | ACCESSIBLE

At The Good Book Company, we are dedicated to helping Christians and local churches grow. We believe that God's growth process always starts with hearing clearly what he has said to us through his timeless word—the Bible.

Ever since we opened our doors in 1991, we have been striving to produce Bible-based resources that bring glory to God. We have grown to become an international provider of user-friendly resources to the Christian community, with believers of all backgrounds and denominations using our books, Bible studies, devotionals, evangelistic resources, and DVD-based courses.

We want to equip ordinary Christians to live for Christ day by day, and churches to grow in their knowledge of God, their love for one another, and the effectiveness of their outreach.

Call us for a discussion of your needs or visit one of our local websites for more information on the resources and services we provide.

Your friends at The Good Book Company

thegoodbook.com | thegoodbook.co.uk
thegoodbook.com.au | thegoodbook.co.nz
thegoodbook.co.in